Welcome to a wonderful, whimsical wintry world!

'Winter Wonder' is designed to keep you warm and cosy during the winter months. There are plenty of woodland animals up to mischief, and of course some old friends drop by. All to help you relax, create and celebrate the season.

So curl up by the fire, have a hot cocoa nearby, grab your colored pencils or markers and enjoy!

See more at rjhampson.com

 russelljamesart   @rjhampson

Published by Hop Skip Jump. PO Box 1324 Buderim Queensland Australia 4556
First published 2025. Copyright © 2025 R.J. Hampson.

All Rights Reserved. Without limiting the rights under copyright reserved above, no part of this publication may be reproduced, stored in or introduced into a retrieval system, or transmitted, in any form or by any means (electronic, mechanical, photocopying, recording or otherwise), without the prior written permission of both the copyright owner and the above publisher of this book. The only exception is by a reviewer who may share short excerpts in a review.

ISBN: 978-1-922472-47-2

Using this book

Find a quiet place away from distractions. Relax and immerse yourself in the process of coloring as you explore the details of each fantastic illustration.

This book is best suited to color pencils or markers. Wet mediums should be used sparingly. Slide a card or sheets of paper behind the illustration you are coloring to avoid marker bleed through.

Find fresh coloring pages by signing up to Russell's newsletter. Get free downloadable pages and updates on new books at -

rjhampson.com

FIRST SNOW

A WARM HEARTH

WINDOW SEAT

LOST IN THE STORY

WHEN AUTUMN LEAVES START TO FALL

GINGERBREAD TOWN

ONE ENCHANTED EVENING

PUMPKIN SPICE LATTE

ICECAPADES

A PUDDLE PROBLEM

A WARM HEART

THE TOYMAKER

SHEEP MAY SAFELY GRAZE

SHOPPING SPREE

REAR WINDOW

BABY IT'S COLD OUTSIDE

UNEXPECTED VISITORS

DREAMING OF A WHITE CHRISTMAS

KITCHEN CHAOS

VERY IMPORTANT DELIVERY

HURRY UP SANTA!

Need more presents under your tree?

Find new coloring pages by signing up to R.J. Hampson's newsletter.
Get free downloadable pages, monthly coloring sheets,
and updates on new books at -

rjhampson.com/coloring

Thanks for choosing this coloring book.
If you enjoyed it, please consider leaving an Amazon review.
It will help to let more people in on the experience
plus you'd certainly make this illustrator very happy!

More books in this series

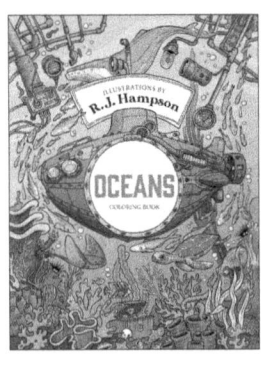    

More books in other series

See flip-throughs for all coloring books at **rjhampson.com**

www.ingramcontent.com/pod-product-compliance
Lightning Source LLC
Chambersburg PA
CBHW042355280426

43661CB00095B/1112